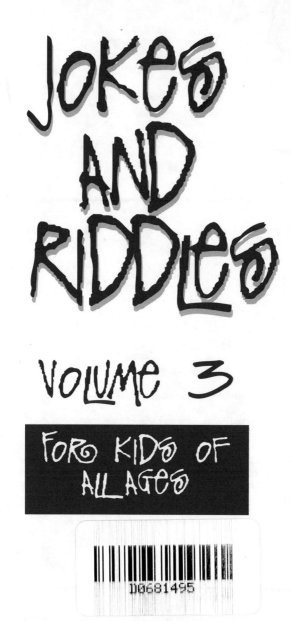

JOKES AND RIDDLES

VOLUME 3

FOR KIDS OF ALL AGES

Jokes & Riddles Volume 3

Copyright © 2005 Sweetwater Press

Produced by Cliff Road Books

ISBN 1-58173-313-5

Book design by Pat Covert
Illustrations by Tim Rocks

Printed in the U.S.

Order books online at www.booksamillion.com

JOKES AND RIDDLES

VOLUME 3

FOR KIDS OF ALL AGES

SWEET WATER PRESS

JOKES AND RIDDLES

VOLUME 3

Q: Which side of the chicken has the most feathers?

A: The outside.

Q: Have you heard about the disease you can get from birds?

A: It's untweetable.

Q: What is the difference between a cat and a comma?

A: One has claws before the paws, and the other has a clause before the pause.

Q: Where do ants
go for vacation?

A: Frants.

Q: What do you get
when two giraffes
collide?

A: A giraffic jam.

Q: What is a frog's favorite game?

A: Croak-et.

Q: WHERE DO BLACK BIRDS GO FOR A DRINK?

A: A CROW BAR.

Q: WHAT BIRDS SPEND ALL THEIR TIME ON THEIR KNEES?

A: BIRDS OF PREY.

Q: WHAT ANIMALS
DO YOU FIND IN
PRISON?

A: JAIL BIRDS.

Q: WHEN IS THE BEST
TIME TO BUY A BIRD?

A: WHEN THEY ARE
GOING CHEAP.

Q: Where do tadpoles change?

A: In a croakroom!

Q: Why are goldfish red?

A: The water turns them rusty!

Q: What do you call a man with cow droppings all over his feet?

A: An nincowpoop!

DOCTOR

JOKES

"Doctor, Doctor!
I swallowed a bone!"
"Are you choking?"
"No, I'm serious!"

"Doctor, Doctor,
I think I need glasses."
"I think you do, too, but this
is a golf shop."

"Doctor, Doctor, I think I'm a bell."
"Take two aspirin, and if you don't feel better, give me a ring."

"Doctor, Doctor, my son swallowed my pen. What should I do?"
"Use a pencil until I get there."

"Doctor, Doctor, I think I'm suffering from déjà vu."

"I think you are, too. Didn't I see you here yesterday?"

"Doctor, Doctor, how do I stop my nose from running?"

"Stick your foot out to trip it up."

"Doctor, Doctor,
I tend to flush a lot."

"Don't worry. It's just a
chain reaction!"

"Doctor, Doctor, I keep
thinking I'm a bee."

"Buzz off, can't you
see I'm busy?"

"Doctor, Doctor, I think there is something wrong with these pills you gave me for my B.O.!"

"What's wrong with them?"

"They keep slipping out from under my arms!"

"Doctor, Doctor,
I feel like a sheep."

"That's
baaaaaaaaaad!"

"Doctor, Doctor,
I keep thinking I'm
a mosquito."

"Go away, sucker!"

"Doctor, Doctor,
everyone keeps
throwing me in the
garbage."

"Don't talk rubbish!"

Q: Who was the first underwater spy?

A: James Pond!

Q: What has forty feet and sings?

A: The school choir!

Q: What is the best hand to write with?

A: Neither - it's best to write with a pen!

Q: When do crows perch on telephone wires?

A: When they want to make a long-distance caw.

"What did you get for Christmas?"

"A mouth organ, and it's the best present I've ever had."

"Why?"

"My mum gives me extra pocket money every week not to play it!"

CHICKEN

JOKES!

Q: HOW DO CHICKENS BAKE A CAKE?

A: FROM SCRATCH.

Q: WHAT DO YOU CALL A BUNCH OF CHICKENS PLAYING HIDE-AND-SEEK?

A: FOWL PLAY.

Q: How many rotten eggs does it take to make a stink bomb?

A: A phew!

Q: What did the chick say when it saw an orange in the nest?

A: "Look at the orange mama laid."

Q: Why do hens lay eggs?

A: If they dropped them, they would break.

Q: Is chicken soup good for your health?

A: Not if you're the chicken.

Q: Why did the farmer frown when he passed the hen house?

A: He heard fowl language.

Diner: "Excuse me, sir, do you serve chicken here?"

Waiter: "Of course! We serve everyone."

Q: How do chickens dance?

A: They much prefer chick to chick.

Q: What do you call a crazy chicken?

A: A cuckoo cluck.

Q: What dance will a chicken not do?

A: The fox trot.

Q: Why does a rooster watch TV?

A: For hen-tertain-ment.

Q: WHAT DO YOU GET IF YOU CROSS A NUN AND A CHICKEN?

A: A PECKING ORDER!

Q: WHAT DO YOU GET WHEN YOU CROSS A CHICKEN WITH A BELL?

A: A BIRD THAT WRINGS ITS OWN NECK.

Q: WHAT DO YOU TELL A CHICKEN AS SHE IS LEAVING THE PARTY?

A: GOOD NIGHT.

Q: Why did George Washington stand up in the boat when crossing the Delaware River?

A: He was afraid if he sat down, someone would give him an oar to row!

Q: What's the name for a short-legged tramp?

A: A low-down bum!

Q: What is the best day of the week to sleep?

A: Snooze-day!

"Tell me," said the tourist to the local yokel. "Will this path take me to the main road?"

"No sir!" replied the man. "You'll have to go by yourself!"

Q: Where do TVs go on vacation?

A: To remote islands.

Q: How do you know when a cat has eaten a goose?

A: It has that down-in-the-mouth look.

Q: What do you get when you cross a cat with a canary?

A: A peeping tom.

Q: WHAT HAPPENED WHEN THE DOG WENT TO THE FLEA CIRCUS?

A: HE STOLE THE SHOW.

Q: What is a volcano?

A: A mountain with hiccups!

Q: Who is the biggest gangster in the sea?

A: Al Caprawn!

Q: WHY DID THE JELLY WOBBLE?

A: IT SAW THE MILK SHAKE.

Q: WHAT ANIMAL DO YOU LOOK LIKE WHEN YOU GET INTO THE BATH?

A: A LITTLE BEAR.

Q: HOW DO YOU HIRE A CLOWN?

A: YOU PUT HIM ON STILTS.

Q: What is a bear's favorite drink?

A: Koka-Koala.

Q: Why do dogs bury their bones in the ground?

A: Because they cannot bury them in trees.

INSECT

JOKES

Q: What does a
queen bee do
after she burps?

A: Issues a royal pardon.

Q: What did the father
spider say to his bad son?

A: You're driving me
up the wall.

Q: What do you get
if you cross ants
with ticks?

A: All sorts of antics.

Q: What game do
elephants like to
play with ants?

A: Squash.

Q: What do you call
an ant from
overseas?

A: Import-ant.

Q: What do ants
take when they are
not feeling well?

A: Ant-ibiotics.

Q: What did the woodworm say to the tree?

A: It's been nice gnawing you.

Q: What is the smallest kind of pillar?

A: A caterpillar.

Q: Why are glow worms good for carrying your bags?

A: Because they can lighten your load.

Q: What do you call a 100 year-old ant?

A: Ant-ique.

Q: Why don't anteaters get sick?

A: They are full of ant-ibodies.

Q: What do you call
a successful ant?

A: An ant-reprenuer.

Q: What kind of
ants are good at
mathematics?

A: Account-ants.

Q: WHO IS A BEE'S FAVORITE SINGER?

A: STING.

Q: WHAT KIND OF GUM DO BEES CHEW?

A: BUMBLE GUM.

Q: WHAT DO YOU CALL A CLUMSY BEE?

A: A FUMBLE BEE.

Q: WHERE DO BEES GET A RIDE?

A: AT THE BUZZ STOP.

Q: What was the snail doing on the highway?

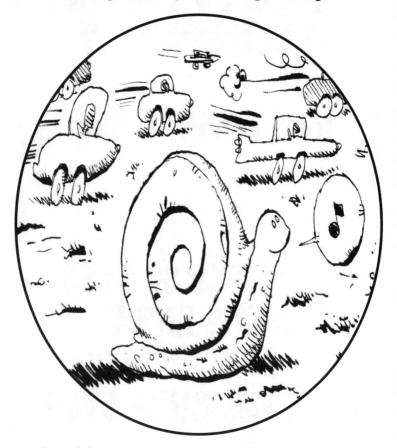

A: About one mile a day.

Q: How would you describe a slug?

A: A snail with a housing problem.

Q: What do you do when two snails are fighting?

A: Let 'em slug it out.

Q: WHAT IS THE BIGGEST MOTH
IN THE WORLD?

A: A WOOLY MAM-MOTH.

Q: WHY WAS THE SMART MOTH
SO UNPOPULAR?

A: HE KEPT PICKING HOLES
IN EVERYTHING.

Q: WHY AREN'T MOTHS
ROCK STARS?

A: A ROLLING STONE GATHERS
NO MOTHS.

Q: WHY DID THE MOTH NIBBLE
A HOLE IN THE CARPET?

A: HE WANTED TO SEE THE
FLOOR SHOW.

Q: HOW DO FIREFLIES
START A RACE?

A: READY, STEADY, GLOW!

Q: WHAT IS THE DIFFERENCE
BETWEEN A GRASSHOPPER
AND A CRICKET?

A: GRASSHOPPERS CAN
PLAY CRICKET,
BUT CRICKETS CANNOT
PLAY GRASSHOPPER.

Q: WHY WAS THE KNIGHT AFRAID OF THE BUG?

A: IT WAS A DRAGONFLY.

Q: WHY WAS THE FIREFLY
ALWAYS STEALING
THINGS?

A: HE WAS LIGHT
FINGERED.

Q: WHAT IS SOOTY AND
WHISTLES WHEN
RUBBING ITS
BACK LEGS TOGETHER?

A: CHIMNEY CRICKET.

Q: What is a mosquito's favorite sport?

A: Skin diving.

Q: Why are mosquitoes religious?

A: They're always preying.

Q: Why did the mosquito go to the dentist?

A: To improve his bite.

Q: What kind of suit does a bee wear to work?

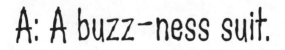

A: A buzz-ness suit.

Q: Why did the fly fly?

A: Because the spider
spied 'er.

Q: What is the frog's best
one-liner?

A: "Pardon me, is this
stool taken?"

Q: What insect runs away from everything?

A: A flee.

Q: How do you find where a flea has bitten you?

A: Start from scratch.

Q: "What's that fly doing in my gravy?"

A: "Looks like the breast stroke!"

Q: Can bees fly in the rain?

A: Not without their little yellow jackets.

Q: What bee is good for your health?

A: A vitamin bee.

Q: What do you get when you cross a bee with a bell?

A: A hum dinger.

"This match won't light!"

"That's funny. It did this morning!"

"I don't think these photographs you've taken do me justice."

"You don't want justice; you want mercy!"

"What do you mean telling everyone that I'm an idiot?"

"I'm sorry, I didn't know it was supposed to be a secret!"

Q: HOW DO YOU KNOW IF AN ELEPHANT IS UNDER YOUR BED?

A: YOUR NOSE TOUCHES THE CEILING.

Q: How do you raise a baby elephant?

A: With a fork lift.

Q: Why is the elephant braver than a hen?

A: Because the elephant isn't chicken.

Q: WHAT IS THE BEST WAY TO SEE A CHARGING HERD OF ELEPHANTS?

A: ON TELEVISION.

Q: WHY DO ELEPHANTS HAVE TRUNKS?

A: BECAUSE THEY WOULD LOOK SILLY WITH GLOVE COMPARTMENTS.

Q: WHY DID THE ELEPHANT EAT A CANDLE?

A: HE WANTED A LIGHT SNACK.

Q: WHAT DO YOU GET WHEN YOU CROSS AN ELEPHANT WITH A KANGAROO?

A: HOLES ALL OVER AUSTRALIA.

"DID YOU HEAR ABOUT THE MAGICIAN WHO USED AN ELEPHANT IN HIS SHOW?"

"NO, I DID NOT."

"THE MAGICIAN RUBBED HIS TRUNK, AND IT TURNED INTO A FOOT LOCKER!"

Q: WHY DO ELEPHANTS DROINK SO MUCH?

A: TO TROY TO FOROGET.

Q: What's the nearest thing to silver?

A: The Lone Ranger's bottom!

Q: What soldiers smell of salt and pepper?

A: Seasoned troopers!

Q: When is the best time to jump on a trampoline?

A: Springtime.

Q: What do elves do after school?

A: Gnome work!

Q: How do we know that the Earth won't come to an end?

A: Because it's round!

Q: What cheese is made backwards?

A: Edam.

Q: How many balls of string would it take to reach the moon?

A: Just one if it's long enough!

Q: What has four legs and an arm?

A: A happy alligator.

Q: How did the shrimp
afford his house?

A: He prawned everything.

Q: What do you get from a
bad-tempered shark?

A: As far away as possible.

Q: What is the lizard's
favorite game?

A: Cricket.

Q: What is a reptile's favorite movie?

A: *The Lizard of Oz*.

Q: Which fish can perform an operation?

A: A sturgeon.

Q: How did the frog die?

A: He kermitted suicide.

Q: What is small, furry,
and good
with a sword?

A: A mouseketeer.

Q: Where do fish go
to borrow money?

A: The loan shark.

Q: What kind of
money do
fishermen make?

A: Net profits.

Q: What is the fastest thing in water?

A: A motor pike!

Q: What kind of fish goes well with toast?

A: Jellyfish.

TEACHER JOKES

"MY TEACHER REMINDS ME OF HISTORY: SHE'S ALWAYS REPEATING HERSELF!"

"GREAT NEWS! TEACHER SAYS WE HAVE A TEST TODAY COME RAIN OR SHINE."

"SO, WHAT'S SO GREAT ABOUT THAT?"

"IT'S SNOWING OUTSIDE!"

Q: How did the boy feel after being caned?

A: Absolutely whacked!

Q: What's black and white all over and difficult?

A: An exam paper.

Q: What's a mushroom?

A: The place they store the school food!

Q: Why was the headmaster worried?

A: There were too many rulers in school!

Q: WHAT KIND OF FOOD DO MATH TEACHERS EAT?

A: SQUARE MEALS!

TEACHER: "WHAT'S 2 AND 2?"

PUPIL: "4."

TEACHER: "THAT'S GOOD."

PUPIL: "GOOD? THAT'S PERFECT!"

TEACHER: "WHO CAN TELL ME WHERE HADRIAN'S WALL IS?"

PUPIL: "I EXPECT IT'S AROUND HADRIAN'S GARDEN!"

Teacher: "Did your parents help you with these homework problems?"
Pupil: "No, I got them all wrong by myself!"

Teacher: "Are you good at math?"
Pupil: "Yes and no."
Teacher: "What do you mean?"
Pupil: "Yes, I'm no good at math!"

Teacher: "What can you tell me about the Dead Sea?"
Pupil: "Did you say he's dead? I didn't even know he was sick!"

Teacher: "I said to draw a cow eating some grass, but you've only drawn the cow."
Pupil: "Yes, the cow ate all the grass!"

"It's clear,"
said the teacher,
"that you haven't
studied your geography.
What's your excuse?"

"well,"
the girl replied,
"My dad says the
world is changing
every day,
so I decided to wait
until it settles down!"

Teacher: "Why did George Washington chop down the cherry tree?"

Pupil: "I'm stumped!"

•

Pupil: "Teacher, I can't solve this problem."

Teacher: "Any five-year-old could solve this one."

Pupil: "Well, no wonder I can't do it, I'm nearly ten!"

Teacher: "I hope I didn't see you looking at Fred's test paper."

Pupil: "I hope you didn't see me either!"

Teacher: "You copied from Fred's exam paper, didn't you?"

Pupil: "How did you know?"

Teacher: "Fred's paper says 'I don't know,' and you have put 'Me neither'!"

Teacher: "Why does the Statue of Liberty stand in New York Harbor?"

Pupil: "Because it can't sit down."

Teacher: "What came after the Stone Age and the Bronze Age?"

Pupil: "The sausage!"

Pupil: "I don't think I deserved a zero on this test!"

Teacher: "I agree, but that's the lowest mark I could give you!"

Teacher: "What family does the octopus belong to?"

Pupil: "Gee, nobody's I know!"

Teacher: 'Why can't you ever answer any of my questions?"

Pupil: "Well, if I could, there wouldn't be much point in my being here!"

Teacher: "That's quite a cough you have there. What are you taking for it?"

Pupil: "I don't know, teacher. What will you give me?"

Teacher: "You aren't paying attention to me. Are you having trouble hearing?"

Pupil: "Not at all, teacher. I'm having trouble listening!"

Teacher: "Class, we will have only half a day of school this morning."

Class: "Hooray!"

Teacher: "We will have the other half this afternoon!"

Teacher: "Now class, I want you to all answer at once. How much is six plus four?"

Class: "At once!"

Teacher: "What's big and yellow and comes in the morning to brighten a mother's day?"

Pupil: "The school bus!"

Teacher: "You missed school yesterday, didn't you?"

Pupil: "Not very much!"

Teacher: "When you yawn, you're supposed to put your hand to your mouth!"

Pupil: "What, and get bitten?"

Teacher: "Didn't you hear me call you?"

Pupil: "But you said not to talk back!"

Teacher: "This is the third time I've had to tell you off this week. What have you got to say about that?"

Pupil: "Thank heavens it's Friday!"

Q: What's the worst thing you're likely to find in the school cafeteria?

A: The food!

TEACHER: WHEN WAS ROME BUILT?

PUPIL: AT NIGHT.

TEACHER: WHY DID YOU SAY THAT?

PUPIL: BECAUSE MY DAD ALWAYS SAYS THAT ROME WASN'T BUILT IN A DAY!

TEACHER: WHERE IS YOUR HOMEWORK?

PUPIL: I PUT IT IN A SAFE, BUT I FORGOT THE COMBINATION!

Q: WHAT IS THE FRUITIEST LESSON?

A: HISTORY, BECAUSE IT'S FULL OF DATES!

Q: WHY DO TEACHERS USE A BAMBOO CANE?

A: BECAUSE WHEN THE CANE GOES "BAM," THE CHILD GOES "BOO!"

LITTLE MONSTER: "I HATE MY TEACHER."

MOTHER MONSTER: "WELL, JUST EAT YOUR SALAD THEN, DEAR!"

TEACHER: "WHY AREN'T YOU DOING VERY WELL IN HISTORY?"

CHILD: "BECAUSE YOU KEEP ASKING ME ABOUT THINGS THAT HAPPENED BEFORE I WAS BORN!"

Q: WHY DID THE TEACHER JUMP IN THE LAKE?

A: SHE WANTED TO TEST THE WATERS.

Q: WHAT DID THE LIPSTICK SAY TO THE TEACHER WHEN SHE MISSED A QUIZ?

A: "CAN I MAKE IT UP?"

PUPIL: "I FAILED EVERY SUBJECT EXCEPT FOR ALGEBRA."

TEACHER: "HOW DID YOU KEEP FROM FAILING THAT?"

PUPIL: "I DIDN'T TAKE IT!"

Q: "WHAT ARE YOU GOING TO BE WHEN YOU GET OUT OF SCHOOL?"

A: "AN OLD MAN!"

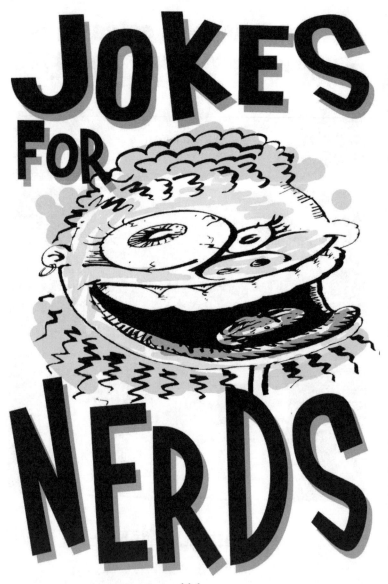

JOKES FOR NERDS

NERD A: "I'M LEARNING ANCIENT HISTORY."

NERD B: "SO AM I; LET'S GO FOR A WALK AND TALK OVER OLD TIMES!"

NERD A: "DO YOU KNOW THE 5TH PRESIDENT OF THE UNITED STATES?"

NERD B: "NO, WE'VE NEVER BEEN INTRODUCED!"

Q: Which Elizabethan sailor could stop bikes?

A: Sir Francis Brake!

Q: How do we know that Joan of Arc was French?

A: She was maid in France!

Q: What is the most dangerous star?

A: A shooting star.

Q: WHEN A KNIGHT IN ARMOR WAS KILLED IN BATTLE, WHAT SIGN DID THEY PUT ON HIS GRAVE?

A: RUST IN PEACE!

Q: WHY WERE THE EARLY DAYS OF HISTORY CALLED THE DARK AGES?

A: BECAUSE THERE WERE SO MANY KNIGHTS!

Q: WHAT DID THE SHERIFF OF NOTTINGHAM SAY WHEN ROBIN HOOD FIRED AT HIM?

A: "WHEW! THAT WAS AN ARROW ESCAPE!"

Nerd A: "I've got a wonder watch. It only cost fifty cents."

Nerd B: "Why is it a wonder watch?"

Nerd A: "Because every time I look at it, I wonder if it is still working."

Nerd A: "Where does success come before work?"

Nerd B: "In the dictionary!"

Nerd A: "Quick, take the steering wheel!"

Nerd B: "Why?"

Nerd A: "Because there is a tree coming straight for us!"

Nerd A: "Did you hear about the fool who keeps going around saying 'no'?"

Nerd B: "No."

Nerd A: "Oh, so it's you!"

Q: What did Noah do while spending time on the ark?

A: Fished, but he didn't catch much. He only had two worms.

Q: How did Noah see the animals in the ark at night?

A: By flood lighting!

Q: What's the moral of the story about Jonah and the whale?

A: You can't keep a good man down!

Q: WHAT WAS CAMELOT FAMOUS FOR?

A: ITS KNIGHT LIFE!

Q: WHEN WAS KING ARTHUR'S ARMY TOO TIRED TO FIGHT?

A: WHEN THEY HAD LOTS OF SLEEPLESS KNIGHTS!

Q: WHO INVENTED KING
ARTHUR'S ROUND TABLE?

A: SIR CUMFERENCE!

Q: WHAT WAS THE FIRST
THING QUEEN ELIZABETH
DID ON ASCENDING TO
THE THRONE?

A: SAT DOWN!

Q: WHAT WOULD
YOU CALL THEFT IN
PEKING?

A: A CHINESE
TAKEAWAY!

Q: WHAT LANGUAGE
DO THEY SPEAK IN
CUBA?

A: CUBIC!

Q: WHAT DO SCOTSMEN EAT?

A: TART 'N' PIE!

Q: WHO WAS THE WORLD'S GREATEST THIEF?

A: ATLAS, BECAUSE HE HELD UP THE WHOLE WORLD!

Q: How was the Roman Empire cut in half?

A: With a pair of caesars!

Q: What did Caesar say to Cleopatra?

A: Toga-ther we can rule the world!

Q: What mouse was a Roman emperor?

A: Julius Cheeser.

Q: What city cheats at exams?

A: Peking!

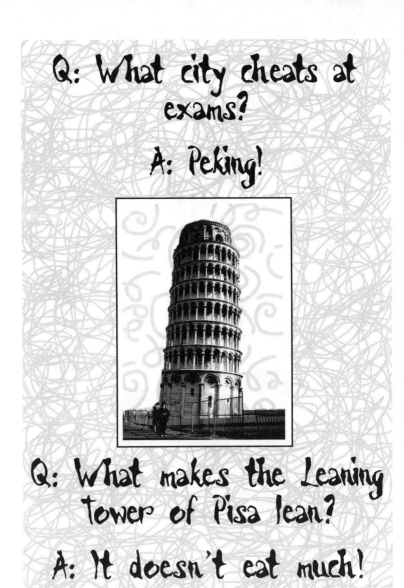

Q: What makes the Leaning Tower of Pisa lean?

A: It doesn't eat much!

Q: Why is Alabama the smartest state in the USA?

A: Because it has 4 A's and one B!

Q: Why did Eve want to move to New York?

A: She fell for the Big Apple!

Q: What followed the dinosaur?

A: Its tail!

Q: Why did the woman take a loaf of bread to bed with her?

A: To feed her nightmare!

Q: Who was the first to invent fire?

A: Some bright spark!

Q: Have you ever seen a duchess?

A: Yes – it's the same as an English "S."

"HAVE YOU EVER SEEN A
MAN-EATING TIGER?"

"NO, BUT I ONCE SAW A MAN
EATING CHICKEN IN THE CAFE
NEXT DOOR!"

"DID YOU HEAR ABOUT THE
MAD SCIENTIST WHO PUT
DYNAMITE IN HIS FRIDGE?"

"THEY SAY IT BLEW HIS COOL!"

"WOULD YOU LIKE A DUCK EGG WITH YOUR TEA?"

"ONLY IF YOU QUACK IT FOR ME!"

"WHO GAVE THE LIBERTY BELL TO PHILADELPHIA?"

"MUST HAVE BEEN A DUCK FAMILY."

"A DUCK FAMILY?"

"DIDN'T YOU SAY THERE WAS A QUACK IN IT?"

Q: WHY DID KING ARTHUR HAVE A ROUND TABLE?

A: SO NO ONE COULD CORNER HIM!

Q: WHAT WAS CAMELOT?

A: A PLACE WHERE PEOPLE PARKED THEIR CAMELS!

Q: WHERE DID KNIGHTS LEARN HOW TO KILL DRAGONS?

A: AT KNIGHT SCHOOL!

q: what animals are on legal documents?

a: seals.

q: what was the greatest accomplishment of the early romans?

a: speaking latin.

q: what tables don't you have to learn?

a: dinner tables.

q: what is it that even the most careful of persons overlooks?

a: his nose.

Q: What is a forum?

A: Two-um plus two-um!

Q: What are the small rivers that run into the Nile?

A: The juve-niles.

Q: Why was the Egyptian girl worried?

A: Because her daddy was a mummy!

Q: What do you call an American drawing?

A: A Yankee doodle!

Q: Why was George Washington buried at Mount Vernon?

A: Because he was dead!

Q: How did the Vikings communicate?

A: By Norse code!

Q: If Atlas supported the world on his shoulders, who supported Atlas?

A: His wife!

Q: WHAT IS CHEDDAR GORGE?

A: A LARGE CHEESE SANDWICH!

Q: WHAT STEPS WOULD YOU TAKE IF A MADMAN CAME AT YOU WITH A KITCHEN KNIFE?

A: GREAT BIG ONES!

Q: WHAT ENGLISH TOWN MAKES BAD SANDWICHES?

A: OLDHAM!

Q: WHY DID THE KNIGHT RUN ABOUT SHOUTING FOR A CAN OPENER?

A: HE HAD A BEE IN HIS SUIT OF ARMOR!

Q: IF IRELAND SANK INTO THE SEA, WHAT COUNTY WOULDN'T SINK?

A: CORK!

Q: HOW DO TELEPHONES GET MARRIED?

A: IN A DOUBLE RING CEREMONY!

ANIMAL JOKES

Q: WHAT DO YOU SAY TO A HITCHHIKING FROG?

A: HOP IN!

Q: WHY ARE FROGS SO HAPPY?

A: THEY EAT WHATEVER BUGS THEM!

Q: WHAT DOES A FROG WEAR ON ST. PATRICK'S DAY?

A: NOTHING!

**Q: WHAT KIND OF SHOES
DO FROGS WEAR?**

A: OPEN TOAD!

**Q: WHAT HAPPENED TO
THE FROG'S CAR WHEN
THE METER EXPIRED?**

A: IT WAS TOAD.

Q: WHAT IS A PARROT'S FAVORITE GAME?

A: HIDE AND GO SPEAK.

Q: WHAT DO YOU CALL A DEAD PARROT AT HIS FUNERAL?

A: A POLYGONE.

Q: Why do polar bears have fur coats?

A: Because they would look silly wearing anoraks!

Q: How do wolves eat their food?

A: They wolf it down.

Q: Why do mother kangaroos hate rainy days?

A: Because the kids have to play inside.

Q: Why don't dolphins
have accidents?

A: Because they do
everything on porpoise.

Q: How do two dolphins
make a decision?

A: They flipper coin.

Q: Who was voted best dressed in the ocean?

A: The swordfish.
He always looks sharp.

Q:
What do sharks eat
with peanut butter?

A:
Jellyfish.

Q:
What do you do
with a blue whale?

A:
Try to cheer him up.

Q: What do you call a wooden fish?

A: A fish stick.

Q: Where can you find chocolate fish?

A: At Cocoa Beach.

Q: What sleeps at the bottom of the sea?

A: A kipper!

Q: How do you communicate with a fish?

A: Drop him a line.

Q: WHAT DO YOU GET WHEN YOU CROSS A CAT WITH A PARROT?

A: A CARROT.

Q: WHAT KIND OF CAT DO YOU NEED WHEN YOU'RE HURT?

A: FIRST AID KITTY.

Q: WHAT DID THE CANARY SAY WHEN ITS NEW CAGE FELL APART?

A: CHEAP! CHEAP!

Q: Why do dogs run in circles?

A: Because it's easier than running in squares.

Q: How do you stop a dog from barking in the back yard?

A: Put it in the front yard.

Q: What do you call a cat wearing shoes?

A: Puss in boots.

Q:
WHY DO TERMITES LOVE FOREST FIRES?

A:
THEY REALLY ENJOY THE BARBECUE.

Q:
WHAT DID THE JUDGE SHOUT WHEN THE SKUNK WAS FOUND GUILTY?

A:
"ODOR IN THE COURT!"

Q:
WHAT IS THE DIFFERENCE BETWEEN A FLEA AND A WOLF?

A:
ONE PROWLS ON THE HAIRY AND THE OTHER HOWLS ON THE PRAIRIE.

Q: What do you call a canary that flies into the pastry dish?

A: A tweety pie.

Q: What did the turkey say before the holiday meal?

A: "I'm stuffed!"

Q: How do you keep a turkey in suspense?

A: I'll let you know tomorrow.

Q: What do you call a bull that tells jokes?

A: Laugha-bull.

Q: Why did the bull rush?

A: Because it saw the cow slip.

Q: What do you call an arctic cow?

A: An eskimoo.

Q:
Where do you get
frog eggs?

A:
At the spawn shop.

Q:
What did the frog say
at the library?

A:
"Read it! Read it! Read it!"

Q: What do you call a frog spy?

A: A croak and dagger agent.

Q: WHAT IS "OUT OF BOUNDS"?

a: an EXHAUSTED KANGAROO!

Q: HOW DO YOU FIX A BROKEN DOWN CHIMP?

A: WITH A MONKEY WRENCH.

Q: WHAT DO YOU CALL A SKUNK THAT FLIES?

A: A SMELLICOPTER.

Q: What kind of snake
is good at math?

A: An adder.

Q: What do you call
a snake working for
the people?

A: A civil serpent.

Q: Why does the ocean roar?

A: You'd roar too if you had crabs on your bottom.

Q: Where do hamsters come from?

A: Hamsterdam!

Q: Who invented underground tunnels?

A: A mole!

Q: What do you call a pig who knows karate?

A: A pork chop.

KNOCK, KNOCK!

JOKES

KNOCK, KNOCK.

WHO'S THERE?

AIDA!

AIDA WHO?

AIDA LOT OF SWEETS

AND NOW I'VE GOT

A TUMMY ACHE!

KNOCK, KNOCK.

WHO'S THERE?

ABBOTT!

ABBOTT WHO?

ABBOTT TIME YOU
ANSWERED THE
DOOR!

KNOCK, KNOCK.

WHO'S THERE?

AARON!

AARON WHO?

I'M AARON ON THE

SIDE OF CAUTION!

Knock, Knock.

Who's there?

Cass!

Cass who?

Cass more flies with

honey than vinegar!

Knock, Knock.

Who's there?

Justice!

Justice who?

Justice as I thought, no one home!

Knock, Knock.

Who's there?

Albee!

Albee who?

Albee a monkey's uncle!

Knock, Knock.

Who's there?

Albert!

Albert who?

Albert you don't know who this is!

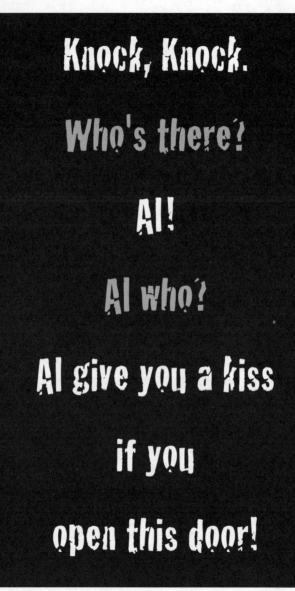

Knock, Knock.

Who's there?

Al!

Al who?

Al give you a kiss

if you

open this door!

Knock, Knock.

Who's there?

Aladdin!

Aladdin who?

Aladdin the street

wants a word

with you!

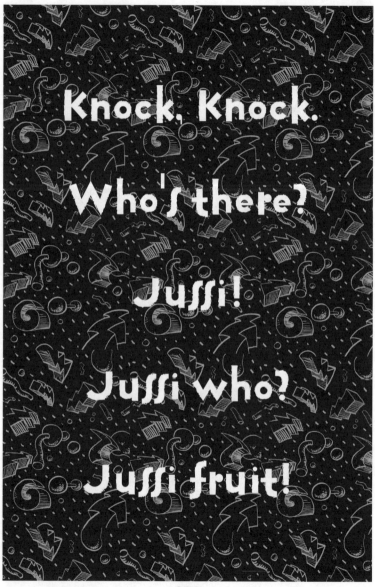

Knock, Knock.

Who's there?

Jussi!

Jussi who?

Jussi fruit!

Knock, Knock.

Who's there?

Jupiter!

Jupiter who?

Jupiter fly in my

soup?

Knock, Knock.

Who's there?

Cash!

Cash who?

I knew you were nuts!

Knock, Knock.

Who's there?

Alex!

Alex who?

Alex the questions around here!

Knock, Knock.

Who's there?

Ada!

Ada who?

Ada burger for

lunch!

Knock, Knock.

Who's there?

Adair!

Adair who?

Adair once but I'm bald now!

KNOCK, KNOCK.

WHO'S THERE?

CASSIE!

CASSIE WHO?

CASSIE THE FOREST FOR THE TREES!

KNOCK, KNOCK.

WHO'S THERE?

ALASKA!

ALASKA WHO?

ALASKA MY FRIEND

THE QUESTION

THEN!

Knock, Knock.

Who's there?

Juno!

Juno who?

Juno what time
it is?

Knock, Knock.

Who's there?

Acid!

Acid who?

Acid down and be quiet!

KEEPING IT IN THE FAMILY!

MOTHER:
"ABRAHAM LINCOLN
HAD A HARD CHILDHOOD.
HE HAD TO WALK SEVEN MILES
TO SCHOOL EVERYDAY."

CHILD:
"WELL, HE SHOULD HAVE
GOTTEN UP EARLIER AND
CAUGHT THE SCHOOL BUS
LIKE EVERYONE ELSE!"

Mother:
"What did you learn in school today?"

Son:
"How to write."

Mother:
"What did you write?"

Son:
"I don't know. They haven't taught us how to read yet!"

Son:
"Dad, can you help me find the lowest common denominator in this problem, please?"

Father:
"Don't tell me that they haven't found it yet; I remember looking for it when I was a boy!"

Mother:
"How was your first
day at school?"

Son:
"It was all right
except for some man
called 'Teacher'
who kept spoiling all
our fun!"

Mother: "Why did you swallow the money I gave you?"

Son: "Well, you did say it was my lunch money!"

Mother:
"Eat your spinach. It'll put color in your cheeks."

Daughter:
"But I don't want green cheeks!"

Little Sis:
"How old is granddaddy?"

Big Sis:
"I don't know, but we've had him a long time!"

Dad:
"It's time for your violin lesson."

Daughter:
"Oh, fiddle!"

Sister:
"What do you get when you cross dad's white paint with his red paint?"

Brother:
"In trouble!"

Son:
"I'm not going back to school ever again."

Father:
"Not going to school...
why not?"

Son:
"The teacher doesn't
know a thing.
All she does is ask
questions!"

Son:
"I can't go to school.

Father:
"Why not?"

Son:
"I don't feel well."

Father:
"Where don't you feel well?"

Son:
"In school!"

Father:
"How were the exam questions?"

Son:
"Easy."

Father:
"Then why do you look so unhappy?"

Son:
"The questions didn't give me any trouble, just the answers!"

"This morning my dad gave me soap flakes instead of corn flakes for breakfast."

"I was so mad, I was foaming at the mouth!"

Dad: "WHAT DID YOU LEARN IN SCHOOL TODAY?"

Son: "NOT ENOUGH. I HAVE TO GO BACK TOMORROW!"

Son: "DAD, THERE IS A MAN AT THE DOOR COLLECTING FOR THE NEW SWIMMING POOL."

Father: "GIVE HIM A GLASS OF WATER!"

FATHER: "I HEAR YOU SKIPPED SCHOOL TO PLAY FOOTBALL."

SON: "NO, I DIDN'T, AND I HAVE THE FISH TO PROVE IT!"

MOTHER: "WHAT WAS THE FIRST THING YOU LEARNED IN CLASS?"

DAUGHTER: "HOW TO TALK WITHOUT MOVING MY LIPS."

JOKES, JOKES, & MORE JOKES!

Q: How do you start a fire with two sticks?

A: Make sure one of them is a match.

Q: What is the difference between bread and the sun?

A: The sun rises from the east, and bread rises from the yeast.

Q: What pet makes the loudest noise?

A: A trum-pet!

Q: Why did the lazy man want a job in a bakery?

A: So he could loaf around!

Q: What do parasites eat for breakfast?

A: Buttered host!

Q: What do you call a foreign body in a pan?

A: An unidentified frying object!

Q: WHY IS A STONE BRAVE?

A: BECAUSE IT IS A LITTLE BOULDER.

Q: WHAT DO YOU GET IF YOU CROSS A CROCODILE WITH A FLOWER?

A: I DON'T KNOW, BUT YOU DON'T WANT TO SMELL IT!

Q: WHAT DO ELVES MAKE SANDWICHES WITH?

A: SHORTBREAD.

Q: WHY DIDN'T THE BANANA SNORE?

A: BECAUSE IT DIDN'T WANT TO WAKE UP THE REST OF THE BUNCH!

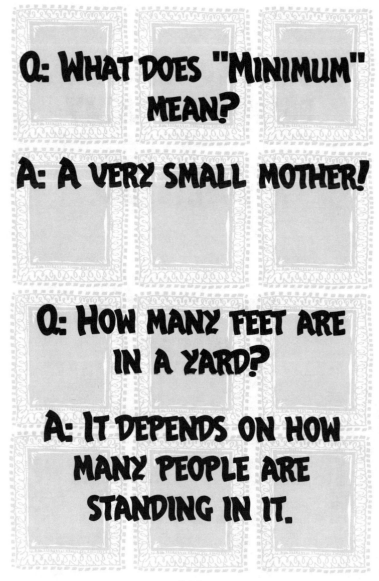

Q: What does "Minimum" mean?

A: A very small mother!

Q: How many feet are in a yard?

A: It depends on how many people are standing in it.

Q: WHAT DOES "MAXIMUM" MEAN?

A: A VERY BIG MOTHER!

Q: Why did the king go to the dentist?

A: To get his teeth crowned!

Q: Why did cavemen draw pictures of hippos and rhinos on their walls?

A: Because they couldn't spell their names!

Q: What happened when the wheel was invented?

A: It caused a revolution!

Q: What is the noisiest game?

A: Squash - because you can't play it without raising a racquet!

Q: WHY DID THE STUPID RACING DRIVER MAKE TEN PIT STOPS DURING THE RACE?

A: HE WAS ASKING FOR DIRECTIONS!

Q: WHAT'S RED AND FLIES AND WOBBLES AT THE SAME TIME?

A: A JELLY COPTER!

Q: HOW DO YOU CURE A HEADACHE?

A: JUST PUT YOUR HEAD THROUGH A WINDOW, AND THE PANE WILL DISAPPEAR!

"DO YOU HAVE ANY INVISIBLE INK?"
"CERTAINLY SIR. WHAT COLOR?"

"HOW IS BUSINESS GOING?"

"I'M LOOKING FOR A NEW CASHIER."

"BUT YOU HAD A NEW ONE ONLY
LAST WEEK."

"YES, I DID. THAT'S THE ONE I'M
LOOKING FOR!"

"I WANT A HAIR CUT PLEASE."
"CERTAINLY, WHICH ONE?"

"DID YOU HEAR ABOUT THE
MAD SCIENTIST WHO INVENTED A
GAS THAT COULD BURN THROUGH
ANYTHING?"

"NO."

"NOW HE'S TRYING TO INVENT
SOMETHING TO KEEP IT IN."

"Do you look in the mirror after you've washed your face?"

"No, I look into a towel!"

"I was once in a play called *Breakfast in Bed*."

"Did you have a big role?"

"No, just toast and jelly!"

"Did you hear about the man who had B.O. on one side only?"

"He bought Right Guard, but couldn't find any Left Guard!"

Q: What is hairy and coughs?

A: A coconut with a cold!

Q: What is the best thing to take into the desert?

A: A thirst aid kit!

Q: What key went to college?

A: Yale!

Q: What did one virus say to another?

A: Stay away! I think I've got penicillin!

"IT'S GONE FOREVER
I TELL YOU!"

"WHAT HAS?"

"YESTERDAY!"

"YOU'RE UGLY."

"YOU'RE DRUNK!"

"YES, BUT IN THE
MORNING I'LL BE
SOBER!"

"A noise woke me up this morning."

"What noise was that?"

"The crack of dawn!"

Q: How do you keep a cold from getting to your chest?

A: Tie a knot in your neck!

Q: Do you know the time?

A: No, I don't believe we've met yet!

"Is this a secondhand shop?"

"Yes sir."

"Good. Can you fit one to my watch then, please!"

Q: Why did the sword swallower swallow an umbrella?

A: He wanted to put something away for a rainy day!

Q: What did Noah do for a job?

A: He was an arkitect.

Q: How do crazy people go through the rain forest?

A: They take the psycho path.

Q: WHERE DOES SEAWEED GO TO LOOK FOR A JOB?

A: IN THE KELP-WANTED ADS.

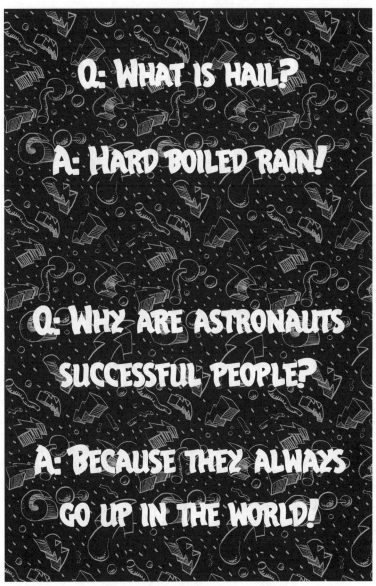

Q: WHAT IS HAIL?

A: HARD BOILED RAIN!

Q: WHY ARE ASTRONAUTS SUCCESSFUL PEOPLE?

A: BECAUSE THEY ALWAYS GO UP IN THE WORLD!

Q: What can you serve but never eat?

A: A volleyball.

Q: Why did the boy sprinkle sugar on his pillow?

A: He wanted sweet dreams.

Q: What kind of shoes do spies wear?

A: Sneakers.

Q: What did one penny say to the other penny?

A: "We make perfect cents."

Q: WHY DID THE COWBOY DIE WITH HIS BOOTS ON?

A: BECAUSE HE DIDN'T WANT TO STUB HIS TOE WHEN HE KICKED THE BUCKET!

Q: WHAT HAS A BOTTOM AT THE TOP?

A: YOUR LEGS!

Q: IF ATHLETES GET ATHLETE'S FOOT, WHAT DO ASTRONAUTS GET?

A: MISSILE TOE!

Q: Where was the Magna Carta signed?

A: At the bottom!

Q: What holds the sun up while it is in the sky?

A: Sunbeams!

Q: Why is perfume
obedient?

A: Because it is scent
wherever it goes!

Q: Why doesn't the sea
spill over the earth?

A: Because it's tide!

Q: Why was the musician arrested?

A: Because he got in treble.

Q: Why do basketball players love cookies?

A: Because they can dunk 'em.

Q: Which food is essential to good music?

A: The beet.

Q: Who gave the little boy a case of the Egyptian flu?

A: His mummy.

Q: Why did the boxer wear gloves to bed?

A: He wanted to hit the sack.

Q: Why did the robber wear blue gloves?

A: He didn't want to get caught red-handed.

Q: Why did the ballerina quit ballet?

A: Because it was tutu hard.

Q: What do you call a cop who never gets out of bed?

A: An undercover police officer.

Q: WHAT DOES ONE STAR SAY TO ANOTHER STAR WHEN THEY MEET?

a: "GLAD TO METEOR!"

Q: WHAT DID THE ALIEN SAY TO THE PUZZLE?

A: "I COME IN PEACE. YOU COME IN PIECES."

Q: WHAT DID THE ALIEN SAY TO THE GARDEN?

A: "TAKE ME TO YOUR WEEDER."

Q: What did the can say to the can opener?

A: "You make me flip my lid."

"How did your mum know you hadn't washed your face?"

"I forgot to wet the soap!"

Q: Which month do soldiers hate most?

A: March.

"Can you use green and pink and yellow in a sentence?"

"When the phone goes green, I pink it up and say yellow."

Q: How can you afford a sand castle?

A: By saving your sand dollars.

Q: What do you do around a blind shark?

A: Keep an eye out!

Q: How do you
talk to a fish?

A: With your mouth.

Q: What do sharks eat
with salesmen?

A: Sell-fish.

Q: Who always forgets where she puts things?

A: Miss Place.

Q: Why were Mrs. Grape and Mr. Grape so happy?

A: They enjoyed raisin kids.

Mr. Smith: "I hate to tell you, but your wife just fell down the wishing well."

Mr. Brown: "Hey, it works!"

Q: Where is Timbuktu?

A: Between Timbukone and Timbukthree.

Q: Why was the water fountain taken to court?

A: It was drunken public.

Q: Why did the girl sit on her watch?

A: So she could be on time.

Q: Why do most cities have the same stores?

A: It's a mall world!

Q: What do you call a broken boomerang?

A: A stick.

Q: What do babies like to ride at amusement parks?

A: Stroller coasters.

Q: Did you take a bath this morning?

A: No, is one missing?

Q: Do you want to hear a construction joke?

A: Sorry, I'm still working on it.

Q: WHAT IS GREEN AND HAS FOUR LEGS AND TWO TRUNKS?

A: TWO SEASICK TOURISTS!

Q: WHAT DO YOU CALL A SICK EAGLE?

A: ILL-EAGLE.

Q: WHAT DO YOU CALL TWO DOCTORS?

A: A PAIR OF MEDICS.

Q: WHERE DID THE HAMBURGER TAKE HIS DATE?

A: TO THE MEAT BALL.

Q: WHAT BIRD IS GOOD AT MAKING BREAD?

A: A DOUGH DOUGH.

Q: WHAT DO YOU CALL A FLYING PIE?

A: A MAGPIE.

Q: WHERE IS THE BEST PLACE TO STORE LEFTOVER PIE?

A: IN YOUR STOMACH.

Q: How many lemons grow on trees?

A: All of them.

Q: Why does the milking stool have only three legs?

A: Because the cow has the udder.

Q: How do you make a walnut laugh?

A: Crack it up.

Q: Why did the best man bring bread to the wedding reception?

A: He wanted to make a toast.

Q: What is the most popular game played while shopping?

A: Price-tag.

Q: What did summer say to spring?

A: "Help! I'm think I'm going to fall!"

Q: What do you call being struck by lightning?

A: A shocking experience.

Q: WHO ARE THE YOUNGEST MEMBERS OF THE ARMY?

A: THE INFANTRY.

Q: WHY ARE THERE FENCES AROUND CEMETERIES?

A: BECAUSE EVERYONE'S DYING TO GET IN.

Q: WHAT DO YOU GET WHEN YOU PUT A CANDLE IN A SUIT OF ARMOR?

A: A KNIGHT LIGHT.

Q: What did Neptune say to Saturn?

A: "Give me a ring sometime."

Q: Did you hear the one about the spaceship?

A: It was out of this world.

Q: What kind of bus
crossed the ocean?

A: Colum-bus.

Q: What did the limestone
say to the geologist?

A: "Don't take me for
granite."

Q: WHAT DID THE LAWYER NAME HIS DAUGHTER?

A: SUE.

Q: WHAT DID THE MOUNTAIN CLIMBER NAME HIS SON?

A: CLIFF.

Q: WHAT DO CHEERLEADERS DRINK BEFORE THE BIG GAME?

A: ROOT BEER.

Q: Why do boxers tell
the best jokes?

A: They are good at
the punch line.

Q: Where does a judge
eat his lunch?

A: In the food court.

Q: Why did the scarecrow win an award?

A: Because he was out standing in his field.

Q: What do you need to open a door?

A: A closed door.

Q: What is green and pecks at trees?

A: A wood pickle.

Q: What is the richest kind of air?

A: A billion-air.

Q: What happens to tires when they get old?

A: They retire.

Q: What did the dog get when he graduated from school?

A: A pedigree.

Q: What do jokes and pencils have in common?

A: They're both no good without a point.

Q: How do you get straight A's in school?

A: By using a ruler.

Q: Why are there only 18 letters in the alphabet?

A: Because ET ran away in a UFO and the CIA chased him.

q: what kind of pants do
flowers wear?

a: petal pushers.

q: did you hear about the fire
at the circus?

a: the flames were in·tents.

q: what songs do all the
planets sing?

a: nep·tunes.

q: why did the clown wear
loud socks?

a: so his feet wouldn't fall asleep.

Q: WHY ARE MOVIE STARS SO COOL?

A: BECAUSE THEY HAVE SO MANY FANS.

Q: WHAT DID THE TERMITE SAY WHEN HIS FRIEND ATE HIS LUNCH?

A: WOODEN YOU KNOW IT.

Q: WHAT DID THE VACUUM SAY TO THE BROOM?

A: I WISH EVERYONE WOULD STOP PUSHING US AROUND.

Q: WHAT DO YOU CALL A FAMOUS ARCHER?

A: A SHOOTING STAR.

Q: WHY DO FISH GO TO THE LIBRARY?

A: TO LOOK FOR BOOKWORMS.

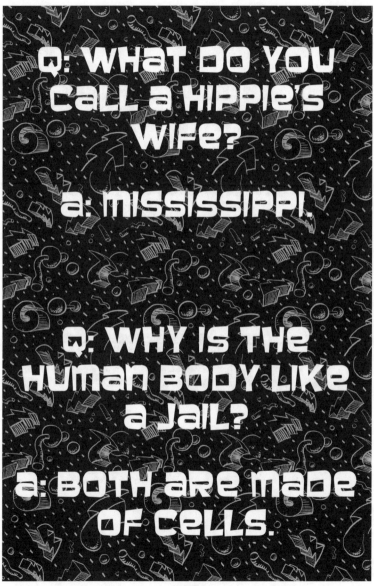

Q: WHAT DO YOU CALL A HIPPIE'S WIFE?

A: MISSISSIPPI.

Q. WHY IS THE HUMAN BODY LIKE A JAIL?

A: BOTH ARE MADE OF CELLS.

Q: WHERE DOES SMART BUTTER GO?

A: ON THE HONOR ROLL.

Q: DID YOU HEAR THE JOKE ABOUT THE ROOF?

A: NEVER MIND, IT'S OVER YOUR HEAD.

Q: WHAT IS ANOTHER NAME FOR A DOG CATCHER?

A: A SPOT REMOVER.

Q: A NICKEL AND DIME WERE ROLLING DOWN A BRIDGE, AND THE NICKEL FELL OFF. WHY?

A: BECAUSE THE DIME HAD MORE CENTS.

THE END!